Das a Baheemyan

Gilbert L. Williams

Copyrights

DAS A BAHEEMYAN Copyright © 2024 by Gilbert L. Williams. All rights reserved. No portion of this book may be reproduced in any form without written permission from the author.

ISBN 9798334690431

Inspire Publishing (Bahamas)

www.InspirePublishing.org

Author Contact:

Gilbert L. Williams

P. O. Box N-696

Nassau, Bahamas

Email: gleroiwill59@gmail.com

REVIEWS

"I absolutely love it. Your spelling gets to the core of Bahamian pronunciation. I am sure dis ain ga be no jook-jook book."

Her Excellency Cheryl Bazard KC
Ambassador Extraordinary and
Plenipotentiary to the Kingdom of Belgium and
the European Union

"I love it!"

Rosemary Clarice Hanna
Musician, Photographer, Community Activist,
Author

"Just read the whole lot, still laughing. Have to read it again ... Well done, Gilbert"

Whitney E. Sands
Computer Technician

"The material I looked at is really impressive and I can't imagine the effort it took to put this book together. I would think this is a treasure and eventually a historical document for The Bahamas!!"

Mark Hayes
President, Civic Relations Group LLC, Seekonk, Massachusetts

ACKNOWLEDGEMENTS

I embrace this opportunity to sincerely acknowledge all those who have assisted and contributed in any way, no matter how small, to the journey of arriving at this destination. While these individuals are too numerous to mention individually, there are a few that I would like to single out for the roles they played. I am awed by the genuine willingness of so many to contribute to someone else's vision and will be forever grateful for our conversations, which ultimately led to you sharing your thoughts and knowledge. My only regret being that not all of you will get to see the finished product.

Special thanks to:

- B. Eloise Armbrister (deceased)
- Roney Armbrister (deceased)
- Mark Hayes

Thank you all from the inner chambers of my heart.

O magnify the Lord
For He is worthy to be praised.

God is good.

DEDICATION

This book is dedicated to the memories of two people that meant the world to me: Berthamae Eloise Armbrister (nee Williams), my mother, and Shaquille Leroy Michael Algernon Williams, my first born.

My mother went to be with her maker in May of 2021, two months after celebrating her 95th birthday. She lived a full life and was able to accomplish and see most (if not all) of what she wanted, enjoying the time spent with her children, grandchildren and great-grandchildren and other family members.

Berthamae Eloise Armbrister (nee Williams)

During her later years, she and her younger sister (Dolores Hanna) would spend countless hours talking about anything and everything. She was truly blessed and was a blessing to many.

Shaquille's departure was very tragic and without warning. In a moment, in the twinkling of an eye. It was also very painful.

Shaquille Leroy Michael Algernon Williams

Shaquille left us in August 2022, just four months shy of his 30th birthday. He possessed a very ambitious entrepreneurial spirit and had embarked on several projects. Unfortunately, and unlike his grandmother, time was not on his side. He was denied the opportunity to see, do, and experience a whole lot of things. Rest assured though, that his time spent here on earth was well spent as he was able to touch and influence many lives.

May their souls rest in eternal peace.

Table of Contents

REVIEWS i
ACKNOWLEDGEMENTS iii
DEDICATION v
INTRODUCTION 1
NATIONAL SYMBOLS OF THE COMMONWEALTH OF THE BAHAMAS 5
BAHEEMYAN VOCABULARY 101 11
BAHEEMYAN VOCABULARY 201 14
DID YOU KNOW 17
DAYS OF DER WEEK 19
I WONDER WHY 21
I WONDER WHY II 23
BAHEEMYAN DELIGHT 25
JOKEY PEOPLE 27
ISLAND TREASURE HUNT 31
FRUITS AN' TINGS 33
DID YOU KNOW II - A FILM MAKER'S PARADISE 35
JUST FOR FUN 38
BOOGIE NIGHTS – BAHEEMYAN STYLE 40
DA GROCERY SHOPPING LIST 44
THE GOOD, THE BAD, THE OUGLY 46
RELL BAHEEMYAN BUFFET 48
I WONDER WHY I WONDER 50

BAHEEMYAN VOCABULARY 301	53
DID YOU KNOW III	55
BAHEEMYAN EXPERIENCE - THINGS BAHEEMYANS SAY, DO OR EXPERIENCE	57
BAHEEMYAN MUSIC IN YA BELLY	59
DAS A BAHEEMYAN	62
BAHAMIAN DISC JOCKEYS ... MASTERS OF THE TURNTABLE	64
NASSAU CENTRIC	66
BAHEEMYAN VOCABULARY – MASTER CLASS	68
FOND MEMORIES	70
WHAT ALL Y'ALL GET BEATIN' WIT?	73
THOSE WERE THE DAYS!	76
DIRECTIONS TO MY HOUSE (BAHEEMYAN STYLE)	80
RELL BAHEEMYAN CHRISTMAS	82
I WONDER IF YOU WONDER WHY!	84
PLACES OF INTEREST/HISTORICAL SITES	86
RELL BAHEEMYAN BUFFET II	88
GO GET MY BELT!	90
A TIME TO RUN	92
DID YOU KNOW IV	95
MOVIE THEATRES THEN AND NOW	97
NASSAU CENTRIC II	100
THE GOOD, THE BAD, THE OUGLY – SEQUEL	102
WAS IT JUST ME?	104
BAHAMIAN SPORTING GREATS	107

BAHEEMYAN VOCABULARY MASTERCLASS II *110*
KEEPIN' IT RELL *113*
ONE MORE THING *115*

INTRODUCTION

"Das A Baheemyan" is a compilation of things Bahamian. Throughout the book, readers will find many varying aspects of Bahamian culture and history displayed and expressed through highlights of its music, food, places of interest and through a brief look back into the days of old. A number of expressions via the Bahamian dialect will also be found sprinkled throughout the book, giving Bahamians and non-Bahamians alike, a taste of our deep and somewhat unique twist on the English language.

While it is not intended by any means to provide a comprehensive and detailed look at any singular aspect of the Bahamian culture, the book is intended to inspire and encourage readers to reflect on the past and think about the future, to bridge generation gaps within and without the family structure by sparking conversations between the young and not so young, and most of all to become a conversation piece among friends, relatives and general associates.

A number of publications by Bahamian historians, writers and cultural enthusiasts have focused on the people aspect of our past and rightly so. "Das A Baheemyan" makes a deliberate attempt to broaden the focus, bringing other aspects of our past and our culture into play. As the readers navigate the pages of this publication, it should become glaringly obvious that there is so much more of our rich culture to be captured and shared by Bahamians from throughout our archipelago.

Each of our Family Islands is unique in many ways, and it will take individuals native to each island to capture such uniqueness and share it with the rest of The Bahamas and indeed the world.

My sincere hope is that other Bahamians—other "ordinary" Bahamians—will look through these pages, see the simplicity of what has been captured, and immediately say to themselves, "I CAN DO THIS!"

Read, enjoy, and become inspired. There is a story in YOU waiting to be told and ONLY YOU can tell it.

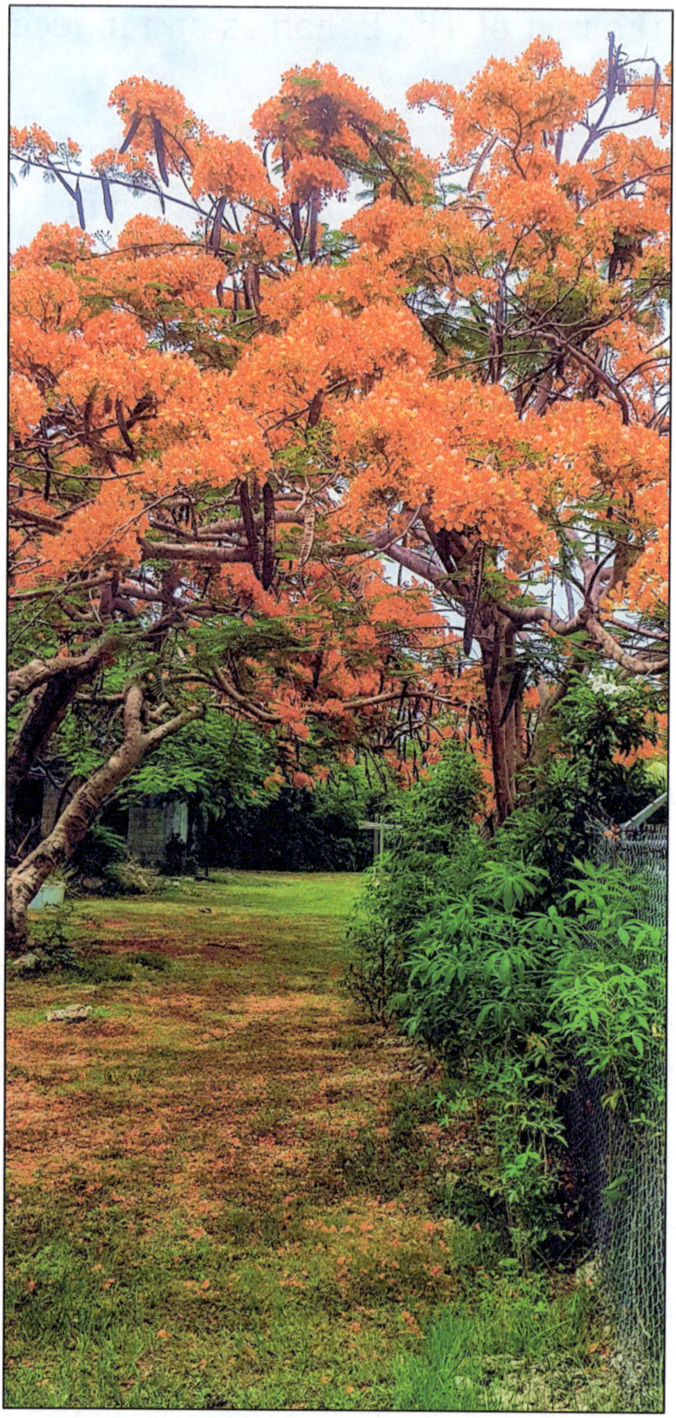

NATIONAL SYMBOLS OF THE COMMONWEALTH OF THE BAHAMAS

National Pledge – Pledge of Allegiance (written by Reverend Dr. Philip Rahming)

I pledge my allegiance to the flag and to the Commonwealth of The Bahamas for which it stands, one people united in love and service.

National Anthem – "March on, Bahamaland" (composed by Timothy Gibson)

Lift up your head to the rising sun Bahamaland;

March on to glory your bright banners waving high.

See how the world marks the manner of your bearing!

Pledge to excel through love and unity.

Pressing onward, march together to a common loftier goal;

Steady sunward, though the weather hide the wide and treacherous shoal.

Lift up your head to the rising sun, Bahamaland;

'Till the road you've trod

Lead unto your God,

March on, Bahamaland.

National Song – "God Bless Our Sunny Clime" (music composed by Timothy Gibson. Words by Reverend Dr. Philip Rahming)

God bless our sunny clime, spur us to height sublime.

To keep men free, let brothers, sisters stand

Firm, trusting hand in hand througout Bahamaland

One brotherhood, one brotherhood.

Late gratefulness ascend, courageous deed extend

from isle to isle. Long let us treasure peace

So may our lives increase, our prayers never cease.

Let freedom ring! Let freedom ring!

The long, long night has passed, the morning breaks at last From shore to shore. Sunrise with golden gleam,

Sons n' daughters, share the dream, for one working team One brotherhood, one brotherhood.

Not for this time nor for this chosen few alone

We pledge ourselves. Live loyal to our God.

Love country, friend and foe, oh help us by thy might

Great God our King! Great God our King!

National Flag

Coat of Arms

National Fish – Blue Marlin

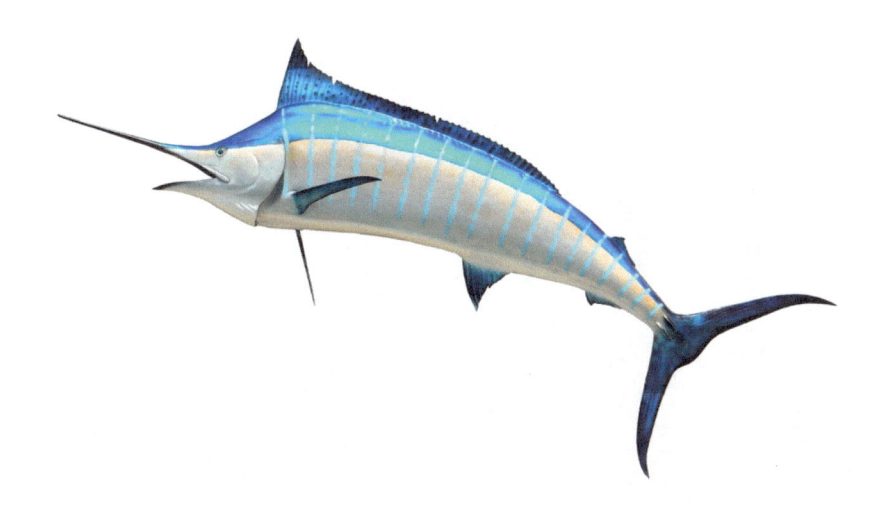

National Bird – Flamingo

National Tree – Lignum Vitae

National Flower – Yellow Elder

BAHEEMYAN VOCABULARY 101

The Bahamian dialect is primarily a spoken language and there is no formal or official written form to accompany it. This makes it somewhat tricky (and maybe intimidating) for some. To add to this, there are any number of different pronunciations (and spellings) for many words as used in the Bahamian dialect. While there are many Bahamians that insist on using/speaking "proper English," there are probably just as many that fully embrace the local dialect during everyday conversation. But what is "proper English" anyway? That's another hour-long debate, at least.

While some people "must" have a cup of coffee first thing in the mornings, there are others that "gatty" have it, some who "gatta" have it, and yes, I personally know a few that "gutty" have it. So there! Who's right? Didn't they all enjoy their morning cup of coffee?

- **NEEM** (Name): Good morning class, my NEEM is Jerry Roker and I from Inagua.
- **AKS** (Ask): If you AKS a silly question you will get a silly answer.
- **BORRY** (Borrow): Go right next door and aks Mr. Brown if I could BORRY he short ladder please.
- **GATTY** (Have to, must): If you really like dat gal you GATTY let her know.
- **DEY** (They): DEY reach too late to catch the 3 o'clock movie. DEY gatty wait for the 5 o'clock showing.
- **DEM** (Them): Go aks DEM if dey ready to go.
- **GERN** (Going): Way you GERN all dress right down to kill?
- **EEN** (Am not, is not, did not, etc.): Dey EEN invite me so I EEN gern.

- **YINNA** (Y'all, you all): YINNA been to the movies last night and een aks me if I wanted to go.
- **KALUNKY** (Oversized, outdated, clunky): Girl way you gern with that big old KALUNKY cell phone? You gatty get one of these new sexy jx63.

BAHEEMYAN VOCABULARY 201

- **PICKY HEAD** (Very short hair mostly on females and not particularly well groomed): You say which one er dem girls I like? Der solid one wit der PICKY HEAD.
- **JOOK** (Poke, stab, pierce and other similar interpretations):
  - We was playing basketball and I miss and JOOK him in his eye.
  - He got into a fight with two guys and one of them JOOK him with a knife.

- **TERLIT** (Toilet, out house, outside toilet): My belly hurting! I need to use the TERLIT before we go.
- **EARL** (Oil): Big man, lemme get three dollars gas and one quart of EARL please.
- **BREKWUS** (Breakfast): Boy hurry eat your BREKWUS and get out of here or you will be late for school.
- **POTCAKE** (Mongrel): I thought you say you had a Collie mix, das a straight up POTCAKE.
- **POT CAKE** (Partially burnt rice left at the bottom of the pot): You want this chicken drumstick with this li'l bit of POT CAKE?
- **TINGUM** (Generic name for someone whose name you can't recall at the moment or just don't know): I'm coming right back. I gern right over by TINGUM to borry his rake.
- **I'ZA** (Short for I is a, I am): Boy I'ZA rell man! I don't take foolishness from nobody.

- **SHUCK** (Shock): Make sure you dry your hands before you plug in the vacuum cleaner or you could get SHUCK.

DID YOU KNOW

- **Did you know that** Paradise Island was previously known as Hog Island and was only accessible by ferry or private boat? In 1966, a bridge connecting the island to New Providence was built, and a second bridge (named the Sir Sidney Poitier Bridge) was added in the late 1990s.
- Did you know that the island now known as Castaway Cay was formerly called Gorda Cay? In 1997, Disney Cruise Lines purchased a 99-year land lease from the Bahamian government and renamed the island Castaway Cay.

- Did you know that the island now known as San Salvador was formerly named Watlings Island, and prior to that was called Guanahani? The name was changed to San Salvador in 1926 after it was supposedly determined by historians that the description of the island best fit the description where Christopher Columbus first made landfall in The Bahamas (this is still the subject of controversy to this day).
- Did you know that the island now known as Cat Island was formerly known as San Salvador? In 1926, the Act known as the Cat Island and San Salvador or Watlings Island Names Act, legally transferred the name San Salvador to "The Island now known as Watlings Island …" This same Act stated that "The Island now generally known as San Salvador or Cat Island shall be called and referred to as Cat Island.

DAYS OF DER WEEK

- Sundee
- Mundee
- Chewsdee
- Wenezdee
- Tursdee
- Frydee
- Satdee

Nah sometimes some people does get mix up 'cause dey does say Mundee is der first day of der week. I know dey gatty be wrong 'cause Chewsdee is der Turd day of der week and

Mundee come right before Chewsdee so it gatty be der second day.

What yinna tink? I right or I wrong?

I WONDER WHY

I wonder why so many Bahamians pay so little attention to certain family members while they are alive, but when those certain family members meet their demise, there seems to be a mad scramble to demonstrate a connection to the deceased. Let's follow:

Girl, you hear Cousin Rannie dead? Dat cause me take bed. Me and him was dead cool ya know. I know he had he li'l ways but I een never had no problem with him except for dat one time when I catch hum trying to break in my car and had to roll him right out. Yeah man, I jess run into him about three weeks ago when I was driving down Market Street. He did aks me for five dollars and if I could give him a ride but I was kinda hurry and I was gern the opposite way so I couldn't give him no ride. I give him two dollars doe 'cause das all der change I had. I had one ten-dollar bill but since he did only aks me for five I didn't wan give him all of dat.

And gal, I jess had to give Penny piece er my mind 'cause she een had my neem in the funeral booklet, talkin' 'bout erry body neem can't fit, and all er Skeebo and Junior dem neem pile up in dere. Her head mussy een hook on right. I tell her if I don't see my neem in dere when we get to the church, she ger find out jess what lobster red for dat day.

I don't know how she get to be running tings no how!

I WONDER WHY II

I wonder why so many Bahamians have a collection of "old broke down" vehicles in the front of their residences! The vehicles are obviously not even close to being in working condition, but for one reason/excuse or another, the owners refuse to get rid of them. Let's follow along:

Big man, you sellin' da black chevy what in front of der yard?

I did plan on gettin' her fix up and puttin' her back on der road, but der right offer could change my mind.

What year dat is, 1992?

92, yeah. She still runnin' good doe. One ring and valve job, a new fuel pump, a master cylinder kit and a set of water plugs and she'll kick right over.

I'll give you three hundred cash right now and my wrecker driver could tow dat by two o'clock today.

Tree hundred? Boss, I jess tell you dat still runnin' good. I can't let dat go fer nuttin' less than nine hundred.

But das a 92 ... Dat over thirty years old! I was ger strip dat fer parts. Een nobody ger give you nine hundred fer dat.

Strip! Parts! Buddy you need to get out my yard before I loose my rotty. Come roun' here talkin fool bout tree hundred dollars. Das chicken feed bey. And don't come back unless you get some sense in ya head.

BAHEEMYAN DELIGHT

What's your pleasure?

Me? I'm a number 10 "fool" – will eat it anywhere, anytime, any style and from almost anyone.

- Johnny cake
- Potato bread
- Banana bread
- Homemade coconut bread
- Corn bread
- Pineapple upside down cake
- Rum cake
- Pineapple tart

- Coconut tart
- Guava duff
- Coconut duff
- Coconut cake
- Guava cheese cake
- Lemon meringue ie
- Coconut jimmy
- Soursop with sweet milk
- Soursop ice cream
- Guava cake with rum sauce
- Benny cake
- Flour cakes

JOKEY PEOPLE

In Da Kanep Tree

Hey girl, long time no see. And why you out here on da porch wit all dis money in your hand, you tryin' to get rob ay? Where you get all dat from anyhow?

Gal, some fellas from tru der corner bet me I couldn't climb one kanep tree and full up one bag wit kanep. You know ya girl ewwa cudda climb ... when I run up in dat tree wit da bag an' start pickin' kanep, all dey mout' drop wide open an' one er dem even fall out.

Girl Peaches ya too fool! Dey only did wan see ya panties.

Well dey get swing den 'cause I een had on none.

My Daddy Better Than Yours!

Bey Junior my daddy jess get one new car yesterday and dat look dead good.

Man, Skeeta you always braggin' 'bout your daddy. I bet dat still don't look as good as my daddy sun roof Cougar doe.

But my daddy house bigger dan your daddy house doe.

Yeah! My daddy could play basketball better than your daddy doe.

Well, my daddy handsomer than your daddy, and he get more girlfriends.

Bey Skeeta dat een nuttin'! My daddy gern to da moon nex week an' he say he ger bring me some moon rock candy.

Well, my daddy gern to da sun and I ger tell him bring me one hot dog and one hot pattie.

You lyin' bey. Een nobody could go to da sun or dey will get all burn up.

You tink I een know dat. You tink my daddy een get no sense ay. He gern in da night after da sun already set.

Service with a Smile

I am starving. Waitress, do you all have a special on today?

No sir, we don't have a special for today but you can order anything from the menu.

Okay, then I'll have the steamed grouper with ...

Een no more grouper.

Hmm, then give me the curried mutton with white rice and cold slaw.

I jess serve the last order of curry mutton to that lady right over there.

So, what all do you have?

We have erryting on the menu except the grouper and curry mutton

Do you have the cracked conch?

Yes sir, see it right there on the menu

So, I'll have the cracked conch with fries, and can I get a cold mango rattler with that please?

Een no mango rattler.

What Fall?

Muddah sick dread, da 402 come right in and I miss dat ay. One mind tell me go get my number dem first and I still gone listen to my girl 'bout drop her to the hair dresser first 'cause she een had no appointment. One woman who used to live right on da side of us tru muddy alley stop me in da mall dis morning and was telling me how her oldest boy daddy get one uncle who have dis lady from Acklins living with him and she ger be 42 on April 2nd – tomorrow. Then when I step outside the mall heading to my car, dis lady who does sell fruits sell me two big, big Haitian mangos fer four dollars! I'ne care what nobody say bey, I ger play dat straight in late Cali fer four dollars an' box it fer six, and I don't wan' my Ma fool wit me when you see me gern to get my numbers.

ISLAND TREASURE HUNT

On Which Island Can I Find ...

- A Green Castle
- Red Bays
- A Black Point
- An Orange Creek
- Pink Flamingos
- Pink Sand
- Green Wood
- A High Rock
- A Hole In The Wall
- A Salt Pond

- A Pirates Well
- An Old Bight
- A Spring City
- A Deep Creek
- A Hard Bargain
- A Hawks Nest
- A Preacher's Cave
- A Spring Point
- A Compass Point
- A Devil's Point

FRUITS AN' TINGS

We are so blessed to be able to grow such a large variety of fruits in The Bahamas, and to grow them so easily. What's your favourite?

- Kanep (guinep)
- Tambrin (tamarind)
- Ju ju
- Sugar apple
- Soursop
- Custard apple
- Mango
- Guava
- Pineapple

- Hog plum
- Scarlet plum
- Coco plum
- Pigeon plum
- Papaya
- Dilly (sapodilla)
- Coconut
- Banana
- Sea grape
- Sugar cane
- Bread fruit

DID YOU KNOW II - A FILM MAKER'S PARADISE

Did You Know that from as far back as the 1940's The islands of The Bahamas were catching the eyes of commercial film makers, and over time, became a real hot spot for the filming of many well-known movies? Without a doubt, the producers of the James Bond series of movies saw The Bahamas as an ideal location and as a result, many of the James Bond movies (at least in part) were filmed in our beautiful paradise. Some of the James Bond movies made in The Bahamas over the years include:

- "Thunderball" (1965)
- "You Only Live Twice" (1967)
- "The Spy Who Loved Me" (1977)
- "For Your Eyes Only" (1981)
- "Never Say Never Again" (1983)
- "Casino Royale" (2006)

Other well-known and popular movies filmed on our shores include:

- "Flipper's New Adventure" (1964)
- "The Day of the Dolphin" (1973)
- "Splash" (1984)
- "Cocoon" (1985)
- "Jaws: The Revenge" (1987)
- "Cocoon: The Return" (1988)
- "My Father the Hero" (1994)
- "Flipper" (1996)
- "Zeus and Roxanne" (1997)
- "Pirates of the Caribbean: Dead Man's Chest" (2006)
- "Pirates of the Caribbean: At World's End" (2007)

- "Why Did I Get Married Too?" (2009) (The movie premier was also hosted in The Bahamas on Paradise Island in 2010.)

There are so many others filmed on our shores so if you haven't seen any or maybe just feeling a little nostalgic, NOW may be a good time to pop the corn, pour the drinks, grab the remote, and take your pick.

JUST FOR FUN

Here are games and fun things from back in the day. Just a few have made it to present day activities.

- Hop scotch
- Marbles
- Skipping rope
- Jacks
- Bat and ball (rounders)
- Pocking
- Hide and seek
- Knock the can

- Old Grady Say
- Hide the stick
- Ring play
- Spinning top/pegging
- Roller skating/scooters
- Making/flying kites
- Board games (Monopoly, Snakes & Ladders, etc.)
- Street racing (sprints and round the block)
- Bike riding
- Musical chairs
- Card games (Remembrance, Go Fish)
- Ma Riddle, Ma Riddle

BOOGIE NIGHTS – BAHEEMYAN STYLE

Back in the day (1960s, 70s, 80s and maybe early 90s), night life in The Bahamas was "jumping" and it seemed like you could find a night spot almost anywhere, and to fit almost any age group and any musical taste. Whether you were a visitor to our shores or a born and bred Bahamian, finding a spot that catered to your liking was just a matter of knowing where to go.

Listed below to assist with your trip down memory lane are just some that immediately came to mind, including a few in Grand Bahama. Amazingly, there are dozens more that I can think of that are not included here. I hope a few of your favourites are listed and if not, see how many more you can come up with.

- Silver Slipper (East St. opposite Lewis St.)
- Chez Paul Meeres (Market and Flemming Sts.)
- Zanzibar (Blue Hill Rd. near King St.)
- Cat & Fiddle (Nassau St.)
- Club 601 (East Bay St.)
- Banana Boat (Farrington Rd.)
- Central Highway Inn (Wulf Rd. opposite Minnie St.)
- Bristo Club (Golden Gates Shopping Center)
- Lion's Den (Nassau St. and Poinciana Drive)
- Conch Shell (Blue Hill Rd.)
- Rainbow Inn (Balfour Ave.)
- Bayside Lounge (off Bay St.)
- WRLX (Freeport)
- Safari Lounge (Freeport)
- Studio 69 (Freeport)

- Lover's Holiday (Fox Hill)
- Kentucky Springs (Fowler St. off Market)
- Family Island Lounge (Soldier Rd. near East St.)
- Poinciana Inn (Bernard Rd.)
- Disco Inferno (Gleneagles – Shirley St.)
- Trade Winds Lounge (Loews Hotel, Paradise Isl.)
- Melting Pot (Montague Hotel, East Bay)
- Out Island Bar (Nassau Beach Hotel, West Bay)
- Rum Keg (Nassau Beach Hotel, West Bay)
- Fore 'N Aft (Emerald Beach Hotel, West Bay)
- The Palace (Elizabeth Ave.)
- Pastiche (Paradise Island (P.I.) Casino)
- Avery's (Adelaide)
- Back Room (Balmoral Beach Hotel, West Bay)
- Fanta-Z (Crystal Palace Casino, West Bay)
- Captain Nemo's (Deveaux St. off Bay St.)
- La Paon (Sheraton P.I.)

- King and Knights (West Bay St.)
- Back Side (West Bay St. behind King and Knights)
- Crow's Nest (Holiday Inn, P.I.)
- Waterloo (East Bay St.)
- Buccaneer Lounge (Lowes Harbour Cove, P.I.)
- Jungle Club (Fox Hill)
- Club Golden Isles (Carmichael Road)
- Sir Rodgers (Ragged Island St.)

DA GROCERY SHOPPING LIST

- ½ lb balooney sawchiss
- ¼ lb hard cheese
- ¼ lb salt beef
- 1 small loaf white bread
- 1lb pig feet
- 1lb pig tail
- 2 tin lard
- 5lb Robin Hood flour
- 1 box hominy grits
- 1 block Kerigold butter
- 1 tin sweet milk
- 2 large can Carnation cream

- 5lbs Mahatma rice
- 1 box cream of wheat
- 1 box Quakers oats
- 5 pack red Kool-Aid
- 1 small Eno fruit salts
- ½ gal. Borden's milk
- 2 bars Lifebuoy soap
- 1 box cheer
- 1 box Epsom salts
- 1 small bleach
- 2 pot scrubbers
- 4 fleshman yeast

THE GOOD, THE BAD, THE OUGLY

Nick names/aliases of some good, some bad and some dead ougly fellas. You know dem, you label dem, but don't call my neem son.

- Boongalar
- Rock Man
- Crazy Horse
- Live Wire
- Nanny Green
- Lord Frog
- Knuckle Head
- Apace

- Stick-A-Toon
- Claw
- Tickler
- Cave Man
- Lion Heart
- Greasy
- Mr. Big Stuff
- Rack-A-Tack
- Kong
- Lee Marvin
- Karooka
- Josey Wales

RELL BAHEEMYAN BUFFET

Y'all does eat or drink any er deese?

- Pea soup and dough
- Okra soup
- Bean soup
- Chicken in da bag
- Barracuda
- Conch fritters
- Conch salad
- Steamed mince crawfish
- Crawfish salad
- Baked bonefish

- Peas 'n' grits and fry fish
- Crack conch
- Curry mutton
- Crab and grits
- Switcha
- Sky juice (leaded or unleaded)
- Coconut water (straight from the coconut)
- Soursop leaf tea
- Fever grass tea
- Love vine

I WONDER WHY I WONDER

I wonder why so many Bahamians will run you down (even in the middle of the night if need be), to borrow something they desperately need – money, luggage, a gardening tool or anything of necessity. They will find you and they will get to you BY ANY MEANS NECESSARY. However, when it is time to return the borrowed item, woe unto the lender. Let's follow along:

Hey Gina, dis me, Aggie. You know da new luggage set you jess buy couple months ago, girl I need to borry dat. I gern away next week on our company convention and you know ya girl gatty be steppin' out in style. Now ya know I'ne get no trans like dat but my cousin who live wit me her li'l girl daddy live right roun' da corner from you and dey makin' back up so she gern by him tomorrow night. I could let her swing by you and pick it up. Yeah, I know you say you gern away end of the month but I ger be back long before then and soon as I unpack, I ger get dem back to you. Tanks girl, I owe you one.

Couple Weeks Later ...

Hello! Hey Gina, yeah, I back. Girl tings been so busy I even een take all my stuff out dem bags yet. Dis da weekend coming you gern away? Gal well you gatty come pick dem suitcase up tomorrow. Catch ya sef nah, you soun' like you tryin' to run hot wit me. Yeah, I know I tell you I was ger get dem back to you but I couldn't find no ride so what you expect for me to do? Well I can't do nuttin' 'bout dat if your car in da shop and, what? What you say? Catch jitney! Nah wait! I always taut your head was bad but now I know you een playin' wit a full deck. Deese your bags and you is da one what travelling on der weekend so you need to come fer deese if you want dem. Tryin' to keep what bags, girl don't go dere ... what you tink I ger do wit deese, eat dem?

And furthermore, deese mussy was knock off bran neem 'cause one of der wheels dem broke off der middle size bag.

BAHEEMYAN VOCABULARY 301

1. **Slunk** (To perform a task in a lazy manner. To underperform somewhat deliberately): I een carryin' him on no more job wit us. He too like ter SLUNK but when pay day come he is the first one on da line.
2. **GEEN** (Giving): You could beg much as you want, I een GEEN you none.
3. **SUDGE, SUDGY** (Suds, sudsy, frothy): Man, das way too much joy you usin'. Nah you gone make da water too SUDGY.
4. **JESS** (Just): I JESS talk to Sally li'l while ago and she say we must pick her up when we gern.

5. **WUDDA** (Would have): If I did know dat was your brudder I WUDDA let him use my basketball.

6. **ENT** (Isn't, wasn't, didn't, etc.):
    a. George, ENT das ya gal over dere wit da green wigs on her head?
    b. **ENT** Sally gone already? Well, why she aks Peaches dem to pick her up?

7. **RELL** (Real): No bey, my girl don't wear no weave! Das her RELL hair.

8. **BURL** (Boil): I gern by Checkers fer brekwus bey, I feel like eating some good BURL fish and Johnny cake.

9. **EWWA** (Ever): Miss, dat was good! Das da best burl fish I EWWA had.

10. **SLAM BAM** (Sandwich usually made with bread and bologna only. If you are real fortunate, you may sometimes get a little mayonnaise and/or mustard): In udder words, BALOONEY SAWCHISS AND BREAD.

DID YOU KNOW III

Did you know that there are two dozen active lighthouses throughout the islands of The Bahamas, with the oldest dating back to the early 1800s?

According to an article released by The Bahamas Ministry of Tourism in 2011, there were some two dozen active lighthouses throughout The Bahamas, with several more that had been decommissioned. The Hog Island Lighthouse, situated on the western tip of Paradise Island was established in 1817 and is the oldest lighthouse in The Bahamas. According to the Tourism article, it is also the oldest surviving lighthouse in the West Indies.

Lighthouses continue to play an important role within the maritime industry all around the world and can vary significantly in height, with lights that can be seen by mariners for many miles off shore.

While most lighthouses have been automated according to the 2011 article, there are kerosene burning, hand-wound lighthouses remaining around the world, with three of them being right here in The Bahamas. The Southwest Point Lighthouse near Matthew Town, Inagua, the Dixon Hill Lighthouse in San Salvador and the Elbow Reef Lighthouse (the red and white candy-striped lighthouse) on Elbow Cay in Hope Town, Abaco, are still manually operated and still attract the attention of visitors.

Other well-known lighthouses in The Bahamas include the lighthouses at Great Stirrup Cay, Berry Islands, Pinder's Point, Grand Bahama and Hole In The Wall, Abaco.

BAHEEMYAN EXPERIENCE - THINGS BAHEEMYANS SAY, DO OR EXPERIENCE

- Dey always "catchin' gapseed."
- Trying to "take bread out people mout'."
- Like to dress up in dey "Sunday go ter meeting" clothes.
- Dey like to "beat up dey gum."
- Dey like to "get on people last nerve."
- Yeah girl, yer lookin' rell "Spankadocious."
- Why she trying to "put mout' on me."
- Dey like to "follow fashion."
- Dey "too like ter show off."

- I comin' "tereckly."
- "I wish he did slap me."
- He's the "spittin' image of he pa."
- Dey too "curry favour."
- "He tink he slick."
- "Gat plenty smart talk in dey mout'."
- "Hog know right where to rub he skin."
- When it dead cold you could believe dey "catching cowboy."
- "She tink her head bad but she een meet up wit der right person yet."
- "When yer play wit puppy, puppy does lick yer mout'."
- Before dey go to junkanoo plenty er dem does get "Kapoonkle right up."

BAHEEMYAN MUSIC IN YA BELLY

I am certain that everyone has their favourite Bahamian song or artist they like listening to. I attempted to list my all-time top 20 favourites but that was not working for me. There are just too many really great tunes for me to select only 20. So, I ended up with a top 40 and even that was not an easy task. To be clear, these are either original Bahamian songs or songs sung and made popular by Bahamian artists.

Perhaps you can do a much better job than I did and come up with a top 20, or even a top 10. I am willing to bet though, that whether you select a top 10 or 20, a few from my list will also be on your list. Here is my top 40 all-time favourites, in no particular order.

- "Bahamian Music" – Dry Bread
- "Eternal Love" – Leon Taylor and the Roosters
- "Pretty Blue Eyes" – Tony Seymour
- "Lovely" – Lovely
- "Send Him Home" – "Sweet Emily" Austin
- "Shame and Scandal" – Count Bernadino
- "When I Die" – Count Bernadino
- "Sponga Move" – Audley Eden
- "You Get Swing" – Geno D.
- "Steady Date" – Swain and The Citations
- "Oh Cat Island" – Phil Stubbs
- "Little Drummer Boy" – Therez Hepburn
- "Start Me Up" – Funky D
- "Uncle Lou" (medley) – Funky D
- "Catch The Crab" – Elon Moxey
- "Carmen" – Eddie Minnis
- "Pepper In The Vaseline" – Ronnie Butler
- "Endlessly" – Ronnie Butler
- "Age Ain't Nothing But A Number" – Ronnie/Count

- "Down Home" – Phil Stubbs
- "Mr. Bus Driver" – Therez Hepburn
- "Bone Fish Foley" – Phil Stubbs
- "Back To The Island" – Bahamen
- "Just Cause She Fat" – KB
- "Inagua" – Geno D
- "Boom Pine Wine" – Roachy
- "Cry Of The Potcake" – Phil Stubbs
- "We Rakin' and We Scrapin'" – Stileet
- "Granny Flying" – Eddie Minnis
- "Tell Ole I een Here" – Veronica Bishop
- "Party In Da Backyard" – Brilanders
- "Diggin' In Ya Boungey" – D Mac
- "If The Good Lord" – Nita Ellis
- "Lick Me Wit Da Riddem" – KB
- "Slam Bam" – Eddie Minnis
- "Jones Oh Jones" – Blind Blake
- "Look What You Do" – Ronnie/Emily
- "You Gat Me Thinking" – Stevie S.
- "Shotgun Wedding" – Ronnie Butler
- "Burma Road" – Ronnie Butler

DAS A BAHEEMYAN

- If you see someone with a plastic bag or a bottle filled with dirt and hanging it in the mango or kanep tree … Das a Baheemyan.

- If you hear one woman on the phone threatening to go down to that insurance place and "take off all my clothes fer yinna" if they don't pay her insurance claim … Das a Baheemyan.

- If You see one woman wearing slippers and walking fast, fast and holding one li'l boy hand and dragging him behind her talking 'bout "I ger march right down to dat school and give dat teacher a piece of my mind" … Das a Baheemyan.

- If you see one fella with two big rocks in his hands, tears running down his cheeks talking 'bout "I ger get him back boy, come 'roun' here slappin' me fer nuttin" ... Das a Baheemyan.

- If you run into a fella on a Sunday evening speaking with an American accent, and you know he just returned from a weekend trip to Florida ... Das a Baheemyan.

- If you leave one gal in the Jungle Club after 1 a.m. on Saturday and you meet her sitting up in the third row in church on Sunday morning ... Das a Baheemyan.

- If you see some fellas sitting around in one yard slamming dominoes dead hard and talking bad to one another ... dey is Baheemyans, but look dead good, 'cause if they have clothes pin all about on their ears, nose and eye lid ... dey een no Baheemyan 'cause Baheemyan fellas scared er pain. Das some udder set of fellas.

- If you hear one fella telling his insurance man "I will collapse all er my policy dem if yinna don't pay me my Christmas boneless" ... Das A Baheemyan.

BAHAMIAN DISC JOCKEYS ... MASTERS OF THE TURNTABLE

When we talk about our favourite night spots and our favourite tunes from back in the day, it could be considered a major oversight if we did not mention our favourite DJs. After all, these are the guys that kept the air waves pumping, the parties jumping and the night spots rocking 'til the wee hours of the morning. They all brought their own styles as some would quietly do their thing, while others would occasionally let you know they were there. Then there were those who insisted on letting it all hang out. Whether they were radio, party or night club DJs, everyone had a favourite and every DJ had their audience.

Here are a few that I recall, some by full name, some by first name and others simply by their handle.

- Nat Saunders
- Jeff Scavella
- Gordon Lowe
- Hubert Gibson
- Tony Williams
- Prince Bodie
- Dr. Lutz
- Nasty Basty
- T.J.
- Juice
- Scooby Doo
- Dr. Boogie
- Gold Digger
- DJ Pat
- Master Mix
- Super Johnson
- Slick Vick
- Mr. Magical
- Fatback
- Naughty

NASSAU CENTRIC

Do You Remember?

- Three Queen's Restaurant
- Christine and Johnny
- Mr. Nottage Shop
- Cliffie's Barber Shop (original location)
- Kentucky Springs
- Taylor's Industries
- Sunshine Twin Theatre
- Week's Bicycle Shop
- Swanks Pizza
- Coral World

- Nassau Seafloor Aquarium
- Keyboard Lounge
- Hardecker Clinic
- Tony Roma's Restaurant
- Hooter's
- Green Shutter's Restaurant
- Nixon's Book Store
- The Capital Studio
- Mother Donaldson Preschool
- Del Jane

BAHEEMYAN VOCABULARY – MASTER CLASS

1. **YONS** (Your own, yours): Who soda dat is in da fridge? Das YONS eh!
2. **SAWCHISS** (Sausage): I feel like eatin' some steam SAWCHISS and yellow grits for brekwus.
3. **KAPOONKLE UP** (Pissy drunk, mess up): Man, me an' ma boys dem been by Flying High bar last night and we get all KAPOONKLE UP.
4. **WAY YOU IS?** (Where are you?): Hey, WAY YOU IS bey? You know how long we been by da car waiting fer you!

5. **NANNY** (Poop): What dat is I smell? Bey you get dog NANNY all about on ya shoe.

6. **RAYCHEER** (Right here): What you mean way I is? I RAYCHEER by da big ju ju tree. Ent das where we 'pose ter meet?

7. **BUCK UP** (Crash, collide, a person walking into another person or object):
    a. He was driving so fast when he turn the corner he BUCK UP right into dat wall.
    b. She was so busy staring at da man wit all dem big muscles she BUCK UP right into da lamp pole.

8. **DUTTY** (Dirty): Nah wait! Way yinna bunch er DUTTY li'l chirren tink yinna gern? Try hard go home to yinna ma and go bade yinna skin, den y'all could come back and watch TV.

9. **TERECKLEY** (Directly, very soon): Almost time ter go. Call Mama Lee and tell her we coming TERECKLEY.

10. **MUSSY** (Must be): I don't know where dey is. Dey MUSSY gone on da basketball court.

FOND MEMORIES

You memba da long, long time?

- Come to der shop! COME TO DER SHOP! *I hear you! You een gatty shout. What you come for anyhow?* Mr Huyler, my mummy say if you could please truss her couple tings till she get pay Frydee? *Truss? Who your ma is boy?* My mummy neem Shirley Jacks. *You mean big Shirl who live in der house in back of Miss Gibson?* Yes, sir. She say she wan one small loaf er bread, one tin er tomato paste, two pack er grape Kool-Aid, 25-cent salty wit plenty hot sauce and 25 cents wort er long boy. *See here. And tell her dat bring her bill up to 13 dollars and 57 cents. And don't come back before Friday.*

- Four li'l chirren dem sleepin' in one bed. Somebody pee and errybody wet right up. Who pee? I'ne know son but I know one ting, it een me 'cause I stop peeing bed long time.

- Das my car. *Das my car.* Das my car. *Das my car. Das my car.* No, das my car. I see dat first. *I say it first doe.* Man, I'ne playin' no more, you too like ter cheat. *Das yer business wit yer bugs bunny teet.* Shet up wit yer gritsy teet. *Yer boon head.* Yer bicycle seat head. *Das why when my daddy bring me cake an' ice cream when he come home I een geen you none.* Okay, das your car. You say it first. You ger gimme some er your cake and ice cream, right? *Yeah. Anyway, I gone home before street light come on.*

- Bey what you lookin' at me for wit yer big eye. *Bey I could look where I wan' look wit yer ougly sef.* Who you callin' ougly? I'll dash you down yer know. *Oh yeah? See me here den. Dash me down if you bad.* Push me den, see if I wouldn't dash you down. *No, you push me first.* No, you push me first. *Okay, see I push you.* Bey dat li'l push. I even een feel dat. You lucky you een push me hard or else I wudda dash you right down on dis hard ground.

- I gern to open my pack er biscuit ter eat right now and I een sharin'. Who beg een gettin' none and who don't aks een want none.

- Mummy say we must share dis bottle of soda. Well, I want mines in da bottle so pour yours out. Here, I dun drink mine. Why you gone put ya mout' to der bottle. Looka all dem crumbs you leave in dere. I'ne want dat no more. Well, I jess will drink all den.

WHAT ALL Y'ALL GET BEATIN' WIT?

Back in the day and well into the 1980s and even the early 1990s, physical (or corporal) punishment was widely administered and accepted as being the norm when younger children and even teens "did wrong" and were to be punished for their actions. Somewhere along the line, corporal punishment became less widespread and would often be the subject of many discussions, especially when the main topic was child abuse. To this very day, there are still many debates regarding corporal punishment in various forms—who should and shouldn't be allowed to administer same and perhaps more importantly, when it is considered to be abuse.

Ask any number of individuals their views on corporal punishment and you will probably end up with close to an even split of persons in favour versus those who are not, along with a similar number of varied explanations as to why it should or should not happen.

Let me state emphatically that I am opposed to all forms of abuse, especially child abuse, be it physical, sexual, mental or any other kind.

Here, I only raise the subject of child abuse as it relates to physical punishment in its various forms. There is absolutely no intention to explore this subject in this publication, as it goes well beyond the scope, expertise and resources of its author.

During the course of my childhood, and that of many of my personal friends and acquaintances, I (like them) was physically punished on many occasions. Those administering my various measures of punishment included several senior members of my family, three (3) different school principals and a senior teacher, including during my time at boarding school in jolly old England.

Without shame, but with lots of remorse, I will tell you that the whooping I got as a young boy from my grandmother after being caught in a lie, still resonates with me to this day. Did I deserve the punishment? I sure did. Did I learn a valuable lesson that day? You better believe I did (even got the opportunity to share that same lesson with one of my sons). Did my grandmother's lesson (whipping) fall into the category of abuse? Absolutely not!

All that being said and in keeping with the spirit of this publication, please let the people know what all y'all get beatin' wit.

1. Hand (big and calloused)
2. Belt
3. Slippers
4. Wooden spoon
5. Headmaster's cane
6. Plastic car track
7. Electrical cord
8. Tamarind switch
9. 12" Ruler
10. Afro comb
11. Skipping rope

THOSE WERE THE DAYS!

- You ewwa gone to the movies when you was supposed to be somewhere else (like Boys' Brigade) and kept checking outside to make sure it wasn't getting dark?
- You ewwa gone outside to play with no shoes on and step in dog nanny and get it all between your toes?
- You ewwa pick up one rock to throw at someone but as it crumbled in your hand you quickly realized it wasn't a rock but dried up dog poop instead?
- Bey, yinna ewwa get one gap up haircut and was so sheem when you gone to school you tell your friends your li'l

brudder did that while you was sleeping?

- You ewwa get in one row at the pump 'bout who bucket was dere first and who next in line?
- You ewwa row wit one of your siblings or cousins when sharing a fruit, chocolate bar or something similar because you got "der li'l half"?
- You ewwa save up your Coca Cola bottle caps and your money so you could go to the Coca Cola movies during the summer? Six caps and 25 cents ... You'll never see that again!
- You ewwa save the box tops from the Kellogg cereal to collect giveaways from one of the wholesale places?
- You ewwa eat sweet milk and bread, especially homemade bread and had the sweet milk running all down your wrist and elbow because you loaded up on the sweet milk?
- You ewwa row wit one of your siblings or cousins 'bout who getting da bowl or who will get to lick da spoon after the cake batter went into the baking pan?

- You ewwa gone play pegging and get yer top split but yer couldn't tell no one 'cause you were told not to play that silly game?
- You ewwa get in a row wit someone in the street and when you get a good distance from dem you start paulting them with rocks?
- You ewwa get shuck wit one er dem old fridge handle and call your brudder or sister and tell dem you put one cup or baggie in the fridge for dem so dey could get shuck too?
- You ewwa get send to the shop and stop round the corner to shoot dice wit der money? Me needer!
- You ewwa suck your teet, cut your eye, cork up your ears or kiss your hip at anybody?
- You ewwa put your glasses on your head and was all over the place looking for them and blaming someone for moving them?
- Junior, don't lie nah! You remember dat time when we gone to dat li'l jook-jook club what does be dark, dark inside but

der music does be jammin', and you end up dancing wit one short solid gal all night? And den when dey turn der lights on yer could see she only had 'bout 20 teet in her mout' – look like 19 was rotten and all was shaky. You een remember dat?

- Finish dis: Horsey in da carriage giddy gup gup …
- Okay since you tink you bad, finish dis one: 1492, Columbus lost he shoe …

Those really were the days!

DIRECTIONS TO MY HOUSE (BAHEEMYAN STYLE)

Yeah, way you is? You say East Street and Wulf Road by Island Luck? Which way you coming from? Okay, nah listen to me good!

Come up East Street like you gern out to Bay Street and keep gern 'til yer reach der first red light but when you reach der light, don't turn dere, keep gern.

Now when you reach der turd corner on der left hand side after you come cross der light, you ger see one place right on der corner what does sell rum an' ting but don't turn dere eeder 'cause das a one way street. Go down to der second corner after dat on der same left hand side and das where you need to turn.

Nah when you turn, you ger see one big Kanep tree in one yard on der left hand side and das how you ger know you tru der right corner. Nah go straight out to annuder red light and turn left. After you turn you ger come to annuder red light li'l ways down but slow down when you gern cross 'cause plenty accident does be right dere.

After you come cross der light look fer one big church on der right-hand side and das where I ger be. No, I don't live dere, but das where you could pick me up from and den I ger show you where I live.

RELL BAHEEMYAN CHRISTMAS

Like most countries around the world, Christmas in The Bahamas is a very special time of year with lots of festivities. While each island in The Bahamas will celebrate this time of year in their own unique way, some things were almost automatic back in the day. How did you celebrate Christmas and what are your favourite memories?

1. Church services
2. Christmas plays
3. Family gatherings
4. Freshly painted homes
5. New linoleum

6. House parties
7. Baked ham with pineapple and cherries
8. Baked/roast turkey with lots of stuffing and cranberry sauce
9. Green peas and rice, potato salad and baked macaroni
10. Pickled beets, fried plantain and cold slaw
11. Boiled fish, stew fish, stew conch
12. Chicken/mutton/pig feet/sheep tongue souse
13. Johnny cake, homemade bread, potato bread
14. Rum cake, carrot cake, pineapple upside down cake, fruit cake
15. Coconut cakes, peanut cakes, benny cakes, flour cakes
16. Family/board games
17. Apple cider, sky juice, eggnog
18. New bicycles, dolls, roller skates, new outfits
19. JUNKANOO

I WONDER IF YOU WONDER WHY!

I wonder why parents, grandparents and other disciplinarians from back in the day would talk to you and even try to hold a conversation with you while punishing you. I sometimes think about this though, and readily admit that it would be really weird to be punished in utter silence ... Think about it.

While you think, let's drop in on a not so silent whooping.

So Mario, tell me why you just reach home from school. Speak up, boy, I can't hear you. It 3:19 and school out since 2:50. Since when it take you 29 whole minutes to reach home? Go get my belt!

Ent I tell you ... when school out ... come straight home ... when school out ... come straight home. You hear what I say? When school out ... come straight home. You hear me? YOU HEAR ME BOY? Well answer me when I talk to you ... Answer me ... when I talk to you. Let my belt go! LET MY BELT GO! Das right, let it go ... let it go. What you raising your hand for? WHAT YOU RAISING YOUR HAND FOR? Oh I see, you tink you's man, you een no man ... you is a boy ... be a boy ... not a man ... be a boy ... not a man. Now go change your clothes and get straight to your homework, and shut dat noise up in my head before I give you sumtin to cry for.

PLACES OF INTEREST/HISTORICAL SITES

Here are a few places every Bahamian and visitor to our country should endeavor to see:

- Fort Montague (Nassau)
- Water Tower/Fort Fincastle (Nassau)
- Fort Charlotte (Nassau)
- Queen's Staircase (Nassau)
- Bahamas National Trust (Nassau)
- Government House, Mount Fitz-William (Nassau)
- Parliament Square (Nassau)
- Adastra Gardens (Nassau)

- Bonefish Pond (Nassau)
- Clifton Heritage Park (Nassau)
- Glass Window Bridge (Eleuthera)
- Preachers Cave (Eleuthera)
- Elbow Reef Lighthouse/Candy Striped Lighthouse (Hope Town, Abaco)
- Green Turtle Cay (Abaco)
- The Hermitage at Mount Alvernia (Cat Island)
- Dixon Hill Lighthouse (San Salvador)
- Dean's Blue Hole (Long Island)
- Pinder's Point Lighthouse (Grand Bahama)
- Garden of the Groves (Grand Bahama)
- Morton's Salt Plant (Inagua)

RELL BAHEEMYAN BUFFET II

- Tuna/sardines and grits
- Corned beef and grits
- Steam sawchiss and grits
- Chicken souse
- Mutton souse
- Pig feet souse
- Sheep tongue souse
- Stew fish
- Stew conch
- Boil fish
- Fire engine (corned beef and white rice)
- Peas and rice

- Crab and rice
- Baked crab
- Crab and dough
- Crab soup
- Steam turtle
- Grilled pork (whole hog)
- Boiled cassava
- Roast corn

GO GET MY BELT!

What All Y'all Get Beatin' For?

- Getting caught in a lie
- Back talking/answering back (never mind 'bout dis one 'cause you wouldn't be reading this)
- Flouncing
- Cutting your eye
- Taking too long to come back from the pump
- Getting in a fight at the pump
- Losing the fight you got in at the pump

- Taking too long to come home from school (aks Mario 'bout dat)
- Taking too long to get back from an errand
- Fighting with a sibling
- Calling a sibling or a cousin an "ill name"
- Stealing fruits off the neighbour's tree
- Playing in the street
- Asking for more food and not eating it all
- Bringing home a BAD report card
- Getting punished at school
- Taking too long to get the belt to beat you wit
- Bringing the wrong belt (you know the right one)
- Holding the belt while getting beating
- Getting cut with broken glass while playing outside with bare feet.

A TIME TO RUN

I am certain you have all heard the phrase, "There's a time and place for everything." Well, back in the day when certain situations came about, it was definitely "a time to run."

Here are just a few such situations that somehow came to my attention. Perhaps you may be aware of a few more.

- If you were a newspaper boy and you just sold your last paper for the morning, and a much older boy shouted to you in a rough and demanding tone, *"Come Here Shorty,"* it was a time to run.

- If you were on the basketball court, the park or anywhere in the vicinity where a fight broke out, and one of the participants of the fight said, *"I gern home and I coming right back,"* this was not the time for curiosity. It was a time to run.
- If you were in or near a dice game (street gambling) and someone shouted, *"five o!" It was a time to run.*
- If you got into a fight with someone from a neighbouring community and then found out that he had four older brothers, and he said, *"I gern to call my big brudder fer you,"* it was time to run.
- If you were around the corner or through the alley playing the blocks, and one of the guys said, "Bey Billy ya mudda coming and she have one switch in her hand and she walking dead fast," it was time to run.
- If you and a couple friends were throwing rocks up in Mr. Bowe's kanep tree and one of the rocks broke his car windshield, it was time to run.
- If you were a teenage girl (16,17,18) and you asked your mother to go to the

school matinee dance on Saturday and she said no, but you devised a scheme and went anyway, and your friend approached you on the dance floor and says, *"Girl, Shelly one woman to the door wit curlers in her hair and she look jess like ya mudda."* Well sweet girl, it's much too late to run so just get on your knees and pray like you've never prayed before.

DID YOU KNOW IV

Did you know that for decades, The Bahamas has been recognized worldwide and has been winning regional and international awards, both for the beauty of our islands and for the talent of our people? From culinary competitions to entertaining and melodious chorale presentations to underwater beauty and satellite images, CARIFTA championships, Olympic gold, world boxing titles and numerous other awards and recognitions.

In October 2021, The Bahamas Ministry of Tourism, Investments and Aviation won top honours in the "Destination Marketing Website" category of the 2021 Travel Weekly

Megellen Awards for its relaunched website, bahamas.com

Log on today and see for yourself what everybody has been raving about.

MOVIE THEATRES THEN AND NOW

How many of these did you attend or even know about?

I ewwa been right ter plenty er dem before yer know! Fer true, true! Cross my heart.

- Hillside Movie Theatre – New Providence (NP) (South of Mortimer Candy Kitchen, eastern side of East Street hill)
- Cinema Theatre – NP (East and Lewis Streets)

- Fortune Movie Theatre – NP (East Street, eastern side North of Cordeaux Avenue,)
- Paul Meeres Theatre – NP (Market and Fleming Streets, behind the Paul Meeres Club)
- Shirley Street Theatre – NP (Shirley Street just east of Okra Hill)
- Wulf Road Theatre – NP (Wulf Road, west of Pine Dale)
- Capitol Theatre – NP (Market Street, opposite Cockburn Street)
- Nassau Theatre – NP (Elizabeth Avenue, Western side, midway between Bay and Shirley Streets)
- Savoy Theatre – NP (Bay Street, north side just east of Frederick Street)
- Sunshine Twin Theatre – NP (Blue Hill Road and Huyler Street East)
- RND Cinema – NP (Prince Charles Shopping Centre)
- RND West – NP (RND Plaza)
- RND Theatre – Marsh Harbour, Abaco
- Galleria Cinemas – NP (Mall at Marathon)

- Carmichael Drive-In Theatre – NP (Carmichael Road, current BFM location)
- Prince Charles Drive-In Theatre – NP (Prince Charles Drive, just east of Cantebury Park)
- Columbus Movie Theatre – Freeport, Grand Bahama
- Freeport Drive-In Theatre – Freeport, Grand Bahama
- Princess Movie Theatre – Governor's Harbour, Eleuthera
- Rock Sound, Movie Theatre – Rock Sound, Eleuthera
- Fusion IMax Theatre - NP (Gladstone Road)

NASSAU CENTRIC II

How many of these places can you recall or even patronized?

- Olive's Guest House
- Palm Tree Takeaway
- Lums Restaurant
- Pedican's Dry Goods
- Froggy Bicycle Shop
- Same Ole Place
- Leo Carey Shop
- Keen Age Variety Store
- Carrols Food Store No. 1

- Lover's Holiday
- Island TV
- Dolphin Hotel
- GR Sweeting
- The Ice House
- Maura's Toy Land
- People's Penny Savings Bank (Original location)
- Bodie Bank
- Stop N Shop
- C & S Food Land
- West Bay Inn Motel

THE GOOD, THE BAD, THE OUGLY – SEQUEL

Dem first set er fellas was so popular we had to go get some more! Who all you know? And don't lie, if he was ougly, say so.

- Buzzard
- Banana
- Snatches
- Monkey Man
- Chicken
- Rat
- Onion
- Creeper

- Ma Pooey
- Pork Head
- Joe Slack
- Spider
- Kung Fu
- Bass Hog
- Gogie
- Slimy
- Magoo
- Boogaloo
- Barabbas
- Blob

WAS IT JUST ME?

Ever heard the saying "Boy you could hear some foolishness when you een listening eh?"

Here are a few such situations that I happened to hear when I wasn't really listening and was wondering, was it just me?

- Bey, check der calendar see what day August Mundee fallin' on dis year. I tink it may be roun' der middle part er der week but I'ne sure.
- Excuse me sir, I would like to speak with the manager please. *I are the manager, how can I help?*

- Boy I so sorry to hear he dead. You een know what he dead from eh? Okay, well give my condolences to der family and if yer find out what he dead from, call me and lemme know.
- Sweet girl, how much fer der five-dollar special?
- What! You fall down and sprain your ankle. Well girl how you manage dat? You wasn't paying attention eh?
- No, sir, I don't have all the pacifics in front of me but I can have the file pulled and call you back this afternoon.
- What you mean he dead! But I jess talk ter him two days ago. What a time.
- No, see, I did mean ter let him run on wit foolishness. I wasn't scared or nuttin'. I did want him put he hand on me. I was prayin' fer him ter slap me or sumtin … Den you wudda see der rell me. Boy you een know me, eh? Hmmph!
- Gal, Sheena, I get one hot li'l piece ter tell yer but yer can't talk it doe, 'cause I'ne pose ter tell no one.
- Bey Ricky, you carrying chicken in der bag, soda and donuts fer ya mudda? Ent

she have diabetes and hypertension? Yeah, and she does plague wit sugar and pressure too. But dis what she tell me bring her.

- Yeah, I ready, y'all wait for me. All I gatty do is wash my face, brush my teet, put on one long pants and one different shirt, spray on li'l bit er cologne, put on my tennis shoes and I good to go … dat only ger take me two minutes.
- Wow! This a really nice picture you take wit me and my lady. Does you frame them or put them in a key ring?

BAHAMIAN SPORTING GREATS

Over the decades and as far back as the 1950s, there have been many great Bahamian sportsmen and women that have done their part to put The Bahamas on the world sporting map. Our athletes have competed against the world's best, and to the delight of the Bahamian people, they have not only beaten the world's best, but in many instances have become the world's best.

Listed below, in no particular order, are just some of these national sports greats. Who is your favourite sports person and/or your favourite sports moment of all time? Maybe you can create a list of your own and how about trying to name a top five or ten all-time greats ... I couldn't, but have fun trying.

- Sir Durward Knowles (Sailing)
- Elisha Obed (Boxing)
- Mark Knowles (Tennis)
- Mychal Thompson (Basketball)
- Rick Fox (Basketball)
- Ed Armbrister (Baseball)
- Andre Rodgers (Baseball)
- Jonquel Jones (Basketball)
- The Golden Girls (Pauline Davis, Chandra Sturrup, Savatheda Fynes, Debbie Ferguson, Eldeece Clarke) (Athletics)
- The Golden Knights (Chris Brown, Michael Mathieu, Demetrius Pinder, Ramon Miller) (Athletics)
- Anthony Carrol (Body Building)
- Shaunae Miller-Uibo (Athletics)
- Steven Gardiner (Athletics)
- Ed Smith (American Football)
- Avard Moncur (Athletics)

- Tonique Williams-Darling (Athletics)
- Frank Rutherford (Athletics)
- Deandre Ayton (Basketball)
- Buddy Hield (Basketball))
- Alpheus Finlayson (Sports Administration)

BAHEEMYAN VOCABULARY MASTERCLASS II

- **TEEF** (Thief): Yer gatty watch him good when he come to yer house. Errybody know he's a TEEF.
- **TEEF** (Steal): Bey gee da man back he wallet. Yer too like TEEF.
- **YUK** (To pull with a jerk, to take away with force): You see how da man try YUK da woman bag off her shoulder? Good ting da security guard was right behind dem.
- **STIDDA** (Instead of, rather than):

- STIDDA you carry two bucket to the pump one time you only carry one. Now you gatty make two trip.
- You gatty play right field today STIDDA me 'cause I twist my ankle yesterday
- **BAHINE** (Behind, bottom, ass): Be careful wit him girl 'cause he may only wan use you den he'll kick yer right in yer BAHINE.
- **BADE/BADE OFF** (Bathe, to take a bath): Wait fer me bey, I only ger be two minutes. I BADE OFF dis morning so I jess gatty wipe off quick, quick.
- **CHILLUN/CHIRREN** (Children): Dis too much CHIRREN walking up and down in der road and school even een out yet ... sumtin mussy gern on.
- **SHEEM** (Shame): Looka da Patsy! Dis her turd time on der buffet line man, she een gat one ounce er SHEEM.
- **PAULT** (To throw multiple objects at an individual or group of individuals, usually stones/rocks): He een pose to slap you up like dat fer nuttin bey. When we reach by dat old car, we ger PAULT him wit rock bey.

- **JOOK-JOOK** (Small, cramped, somewhat insignificant or of little value): Yeah, I could give you a ride home but I ger drop you on der corner 'cause I een driving my new car up tru da li'l JOOK-JOOK corner.

KEEPIN' IT RELL

Yeah ma boy, what der deal is?

Ha'ad go dawg! Erryting cool. What dat is you gat dere?

Dis da new book I jess buy, "Das A Baheemyan" – dis slammin' dread. I jess can't put it down.

Book! Bey stop from jokin'. You know I'ne into no readin' like dat.

Me needer but one er my cousins tell me 'bout dis and dis even sound jess like us. I even learnin' 'bout some tings I didn't know 'bout.

Yeah! You gat me tinkin'. Len me it den.

LEN? Den I gatty be all roun' der place hunting you down ter get dis back. Keep it rell ma boy, go get your own.

Das a Baheemyan fer yer nah! Wan borry but een wan len. I gern ter get my own book and I een wan' my ma ... Wait, I tink I better get two.

Nah das er wibe. We ger link tomorrow.

ONE MORE THING

Thank you for taking the time to read "Das A Baheemyan." Your decision to secure a copy of this book is really appreciated. I would be honored to receive your feedback. If you purchased your copy on Amazon.com, it would be a great help if you could leave an honest review of the book. If you received it as a gift or purchased it locally, please drop me a line with your thoughts. Reviews are immensely valuable to authors as they help more people discover our books. Thank you once again, and I look forward to hearing from you soon!

Gilbert L. Williams

Made in the USA
Columbia, SC
14 August 2024